CURIOUS questions and answers about...

Weather

Words by Philip Steele
Illustrations by Mike Moran

WINDMILL BOOKS

Published in 2022 by Windmill Books,
an Imprint of Rosen Publishing
29 East 21st Street, New York, NY 10010

Cataloging-in-Publication Data

Names: Steele, Philip, author. | Moran, Mike, illustrator.
Title: Weather / written by Philip Steele, illustrated by Mike Moran.
Description: New York : Windmill Books, 2022. | Series: Curious questions and answers about...
Identifiers: ISBN 9781499487824 (pbk.) | ISBN 9781499487848 (library bound) | ISBN 9781499487831 (6 pack) | ISBN 9781499487855 (ebook)
Subjects: LCSH: Weather--Juvenile literature.
Classification: LCC QC981.3 S742 2022 | DDC 551.6--dc23

Manufactured in the United States of America

CPSIA Compliance Information: Batch BS22WM: For Further Information contact Rosen Publishing, New York, New York at 1-800-237-9932

CURIOUS questions and answers about... Weather

Words by Philip Steele

Illustrations by Mike Moran

What is weather?

Earth is surrounded by a layer of air called the atmosphere. The way the atmosphere behaves is always changing. It is these changes that give us the weather, which may be hot, cold, wet, windy, or sunny.

Sun

The atmosphere is filled with moving air and clouds.

Why does weather happen?

The sun is the nearest star to Earth. It is far, far away in space, but its incredible heat warms our planet. This warmth affects the way that air presses against Earth's surface. Differences between cold and warm places create strong winds, as well as currents in the oceans.

Why do seasons change?

As Earth travels around the sun, it is tilted. This means that northern and southern parts lean toward the sun at different times of the year. So when the north part is leaning towards the sun, it is summer there and winter in the southern part.

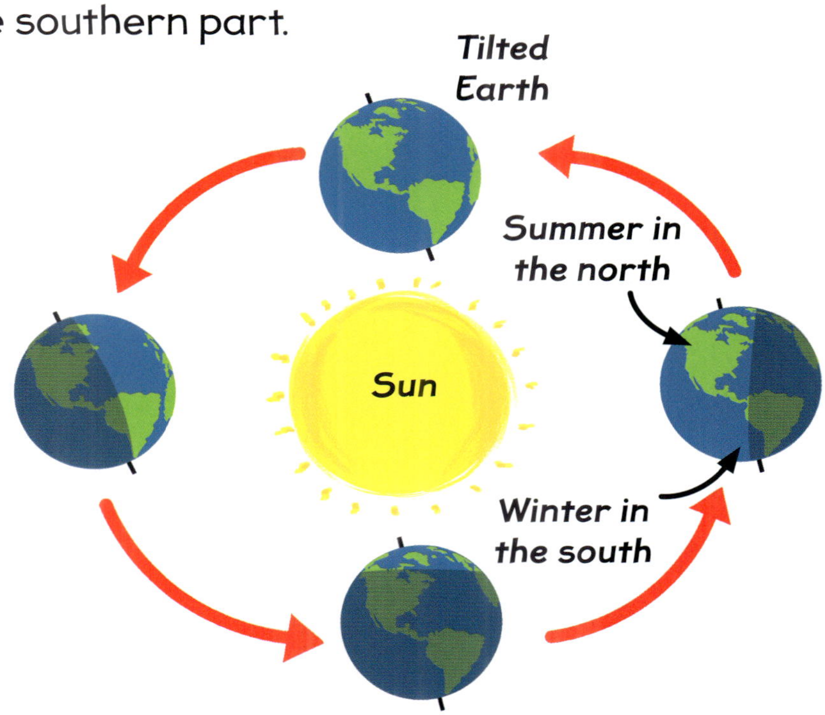

Is weather important?

Yes, it is, because people, animals, and plants need sunshine, warmth, and water to stay alive. However, extreme weather conditions, such as storms or floods, can put lives in danger.

What makes water wonderful?

Water is a liquid. It can freeze to become solid ice. It can turn into a gas called water vapor. Water may change its form, but it lasts forever.

2 It gets gassy

Heat from the sun turns water into a gas called water vapor. This is **evaporation**.

1 There's lots of it!

Over **two-thirds** of Earth's surface is covered in water.

Water is precious

Fresh water keeps us **alive**. Water helps plants grow too. We can wash in it, swim in it, sail on it, and play in it!

3 It rises and cools

As warm water vapor rises, it cools. It **condenses**, turning back into liquid.

4 It makes clouds

Water droplets or solid ice crystals gather around specks of dust and form **clouds**.

5 It falls back down

Water droplets or ice crystals form **raindrops** or **snowflakes**, which fall back to Earth.

6 It goes on and on

Rain and melted snow fill rivers, lakes and oceans, then the whole **water cycle** starts all over again. It helps create our weather.

How hot does it get?

In California's Death Valley, the top temperature ever recorded was over 128°F. A weather satellite has recorded over 158°F in the Lut Desert in Iran.

Where is the driest place on Earth?

The Atacama Desert in Chile. Once, no rain fell there for over 14 years. Long periods without rain are called droughts.

Why do lizards sunbathe?

Reptiles such as lizards are cold-blooded, which means that they can't make their own heat. They bask in the sunshine to warm themselves up.

How can plants survive in a desert?

Some plants have their own water supply. Cacti store water in their thick, spiky stems. Baobab trees store water inside their big, fat trunks.

Why can the sun be a danger?

Where does the weather happen?

In the layer of the atmosphere that is closest to Earth's surface. The atmosphere surrounds our planet like a giant blanket, screening out some harmful rays that come from the sun.

What is a weather system?

Huge masses of air that swirl over Earth's surface are called weather systems. High-pressure systems press air down against the land. They bring drier, clearer weather. Low-pressure systems bring mild or rainy weather. The border between two systems is called a front.

Cirrus

Why do clouds have funny shapes?

Some clouds are white and puffy, and some are thin and streaky. Some pile up like big dark towers, and some form little blobs. Their shape depends on whether they are full of water droplets or ice crystals and how high up they are.

Some clouds look like dragons, castles, or bears in the sky. What can you see up there?

Mackerel sky

Is there a pot of gold at the end of a rainbow?

Only in fairy tales! Rainbows are the most beautiful sights in the sky. Air has no color, but when sunlight passes through rain or mist, the water droplets break up the light into an arc of shimmering colors.

Why does the wind blow?

Because as warm air rises, cold air whooshes in to take its place, and the wind blows! Some winds blow between land and sea. Some cross deserts and mountains. Others blow all the way around the planet.

How does the wind help plants?

Many trees and flowering plants have seeds that are scattered by the wind. Dandelion seeds are light and fluffy and float a long way. Sycamore seeds are like helicopter blades, spinning around.

What is the monsoon?

It is a wind that blows across India. The winter monsoon brings dry weather. In summer it picks up lots of water from the ocean and brings heavy rains to the dry land.

Why do birds ride on the wind?

So we can fly long distances without too much flapping. Over the Southern Ocean, albatrosses like me glide on powerful winds. In South America, condors use currents of warm air to soar above mountains.

How do winds shape rock?

Winds often carry dust, grit, or sand. They blast rocks and cliffs, wearing them down into all sorts of shapes. Water, ice, and heat also shape the surface of planet Earth.

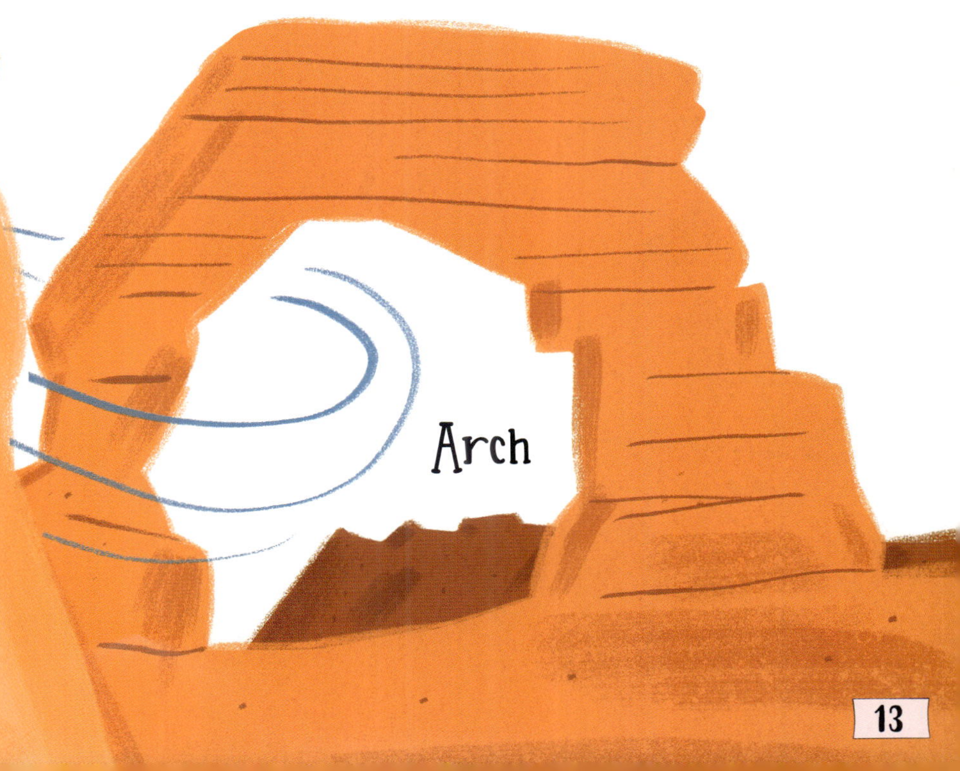

Would you rather?

Go on vacation somewhere **cold** or somewhere **hot**?

Hear crashing **thunder** or see flashes of **lightning**?

Play soccer in the **rain and mud** or during a **heat wave**?

Cruise by boat on a **calm day**...

...or sail on a **windy day**?

Fly **above** the clouds...

Wear a **woolly coat** like a sheep or a **green raincoat** like a tree frog?

Ride on a **surfboard**...

...or a **snowboard?**

Work outside in a **big storm** at sea or inside designing a weather satellite for space?

...or drift **below** the clouds?

What is a hurricane?

It's a terrifying tropical storm, also called a typhoon or a cyclone. A great storm cloud spins around as it sweeps over the ocean. Hurricane-force winds can reach 112 miles an hour or even more.

Is it deadly?

When a hurricane smashes into land, it can be deadly. There are huge waves, heavy rain, floods, and mudslides. Trees can be blown over, homes may be destroyed, and lives may be at risk.

Where is Tornado Alley?

This is an area in the United States that has some of the fiercest whirlwinds of all. They are called tornadoes or twisters. These dark funnels of dust can spin at up to 310 miles an hour. They can suck up a car or even a house.

WATCH OUT!

What is a waterspout?

A whirlwind that forms from warm, moist air over a sea or lake is called a waterspout. It is often joined to the bottom of a cloud.

Why are thunderclouds dark?

Thunderclouds are so full of water droplets that they look very dark. They tower up to 9 miles high.

How do clouds make lightning?

Water vapor rushes up into clouds from the warm ground. Once inside, the vapor cools and freezes, forming balls of ice called hailstones. Air currents ping these up and down inside the cloud, making an electric charge.

BANG!

BOOM!

Thunderstorms can be dangerous.

Why does thunder go bang?

The heat of lightning is incredible, even hotter than the sun. It makes the air expand so fast that it causes a shockwave. BANG!

How fast is lightning?

The electricity connects with the ground or with other clouds, forming a flash of lightning. This can travel nearly 190,000 miles in a single second.

Which comes first, thunder or lightning?

They happen at the same time, but we see the flash first because light travels through the air faster than sound.

Did you know?

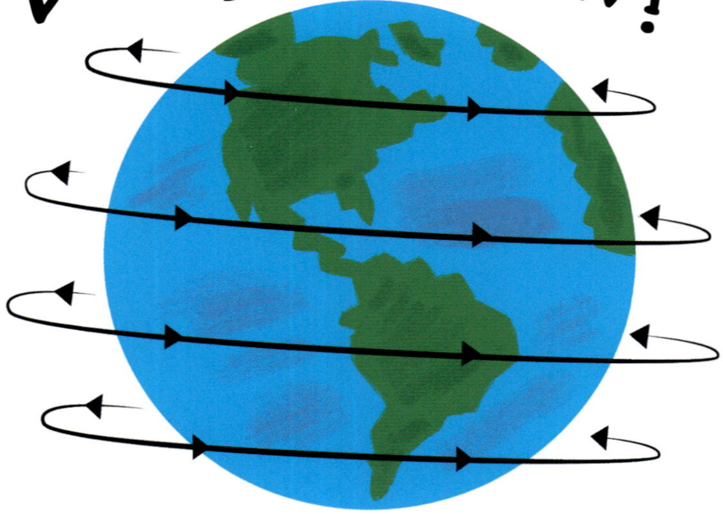

Super-powerful long-distance winds called **jet streams** move along about 6.2 miles above Earth's surface.

The Inuit people of the Arctic can build **igloos** – overnight shelters made from blocks of frozen snow. These are actually quite cozy!

It is said that no two **snowflakes** have exactly the same design!

Fog is just low-level clouds. The Grand Banks off Newfoundland, Canada, have about 206 foggy days each year.

As you are reading these words, there are about 2,000 **thunderstorms** happening around the world.

The spinning of Earth forces **winds** that blow from the poles to the equator to change direction.

COUGH!

When fumes from cars and factories react with sunlight, the air is filled with horrible, poisonous **smog**.

The coats of the **Arctic fox** and **hare** change to white in the winter, so they cannot be seen against the snow.

Fir trees have thin, tough leaves called **needles**, which stay on all winter. These help capture sunlight all year round. They can store water and survive harsh winter storms.

Long ago, people believed that the weather was controlled **by gods and goddesses**. Inti was the Inca sun god. Thor was the Norse god of thunder.

How are snowflakes formed?

When water droplets freeze around specks of dust in a cloud, snowflakes form. These ice crystals freeze more droplets, building up amazing starry shapes and patterns. They stick together to make bigger flakes.

Snowflakes have SIX sides, or points.

What is a blizzard?

A blizzard is a heavy snowstorm driven by high winds. Snow piles up in deep drifts. It's hard to see where you are going as everything looks white!

Why are mountaintops snowy?

Mountaintops are often covered in snow, even in hot countries. The higher you climb, the more the air expands and cools. This leads to more moisture—and snowy mountain conditions.

Where does frost make flowers?

On cold surfaces such as windows, ice, or rock. Ice crystals spread into beautiful patterns that may look like ferns or flowers.

Does the sea ever freeze?

Yes it does, but because the sea contains salt, it has a lower freezing point. It turns to ice below 28.4°F. Freshwater rivers and lakes freeze at 32°F.

How many?

332

The number of days it once rained nonstop on the Hawaiian Island of Oahu!

4,000

The number of hours of sunshine that Yuma, Arizona, receives in a year. It may be the sunniest place on Earth!

The biggest tropical storm ever recorded was a typhoon named Tip, in 1979. It measured **1,379** miles across.

5 years!

That's how long a water-holding frog can go without water during a drought!

37.7 feet: The amount of snow that fell at Tamarack in California during just one day in 1911.

200
The number of miles a single lightning streak ran across the sky above Oklahoma in 2007.

207
The number of tornadoes that happened in a single day in the U.S. in 2011.

8 hours **58** minutes:
The longest-lasting rainbow in Taiwan in 2017.

2.2
The weight in pounds of giant hailstones that fell in Bangladesh in 1986.

–128.6°F
The lowest temperature ever recorded was at the Vostok scientific base in Antarctica in July 1983.

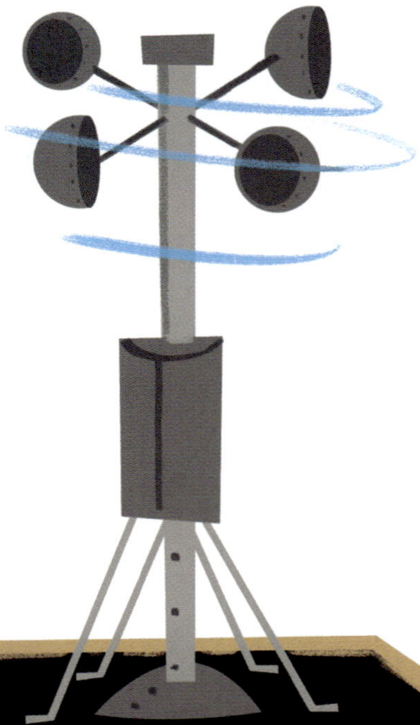

How do we measure the weather?

All sorts of clever gadgets have been invented over the years to measure how the weather behaves. Today, the numbers are often recorded and displayed digitally.

Anemometers measure wind speed. They are often fixed to tall buildings, bridges, and ships.

Rain gauges collect and measure the amount of rain that falls into a jar.

Thermometers measure how hot or cold it gets. The best-known thermometers show how a liquid metal called mercury goes up or down inside a glass tube. Most weather scientists today use electrical resistance thermometers.

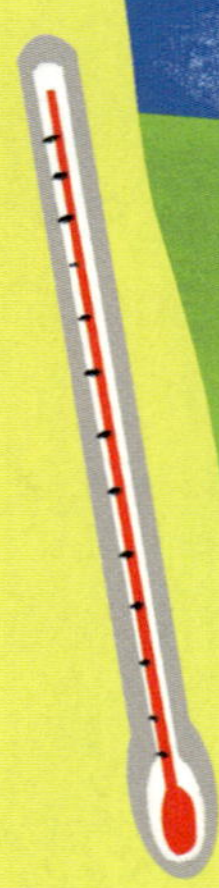

Barometers measure changes in air pressure. There are many different designs and displays.

Weather balloons carry instruments high above Earth to study the atmosphere.

Satellites in space help us collect information about the climate. Buoys and ships at sea also record weather data and so do aircraft.

Does the climate ever change?

Over millions of years, Earth's climate has gone through many changes. In the past, there have been great ice ages when ice spread out from the poles.

Woolly mammoth

What's happening today?

The climate is changing very quickly. This is because we are cutting down forests and burning too much oil, gas, and coal. We are filling the atmosphere with gases that make the planet overheat.

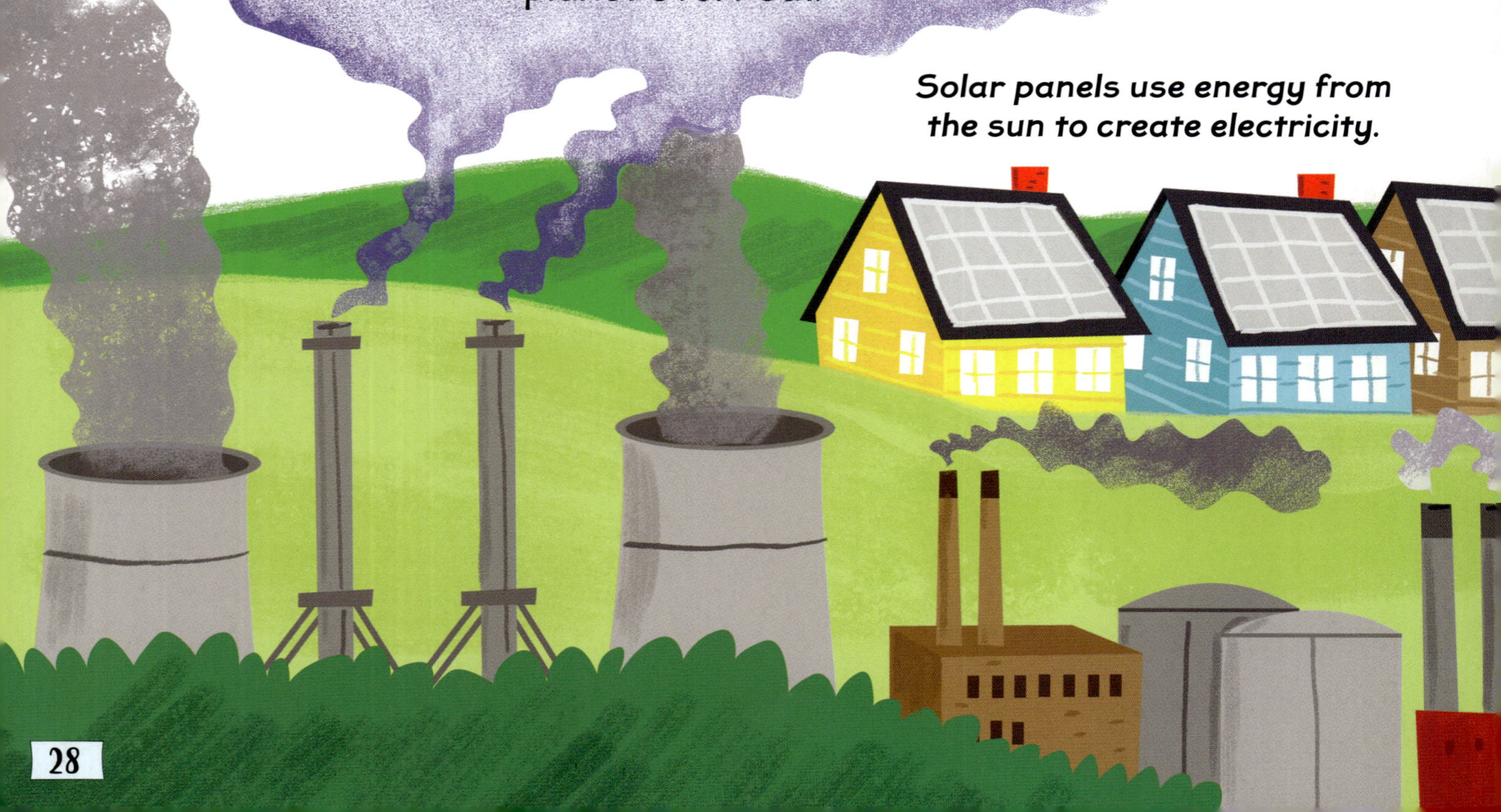

Solar panels use energy from the sun to create electricity.

How will climate change affect the weather?

We may see more big tropical storms, floods in some places and droughts in others, melting ice, and rising sea levels. Dry areas may turn to deserts.

How can the weather help us out?

We can use wind, sunlight, waves, tides, and rivers to make cleaner energy that never runs out. Let's look after our planet—it's the only one we've got!

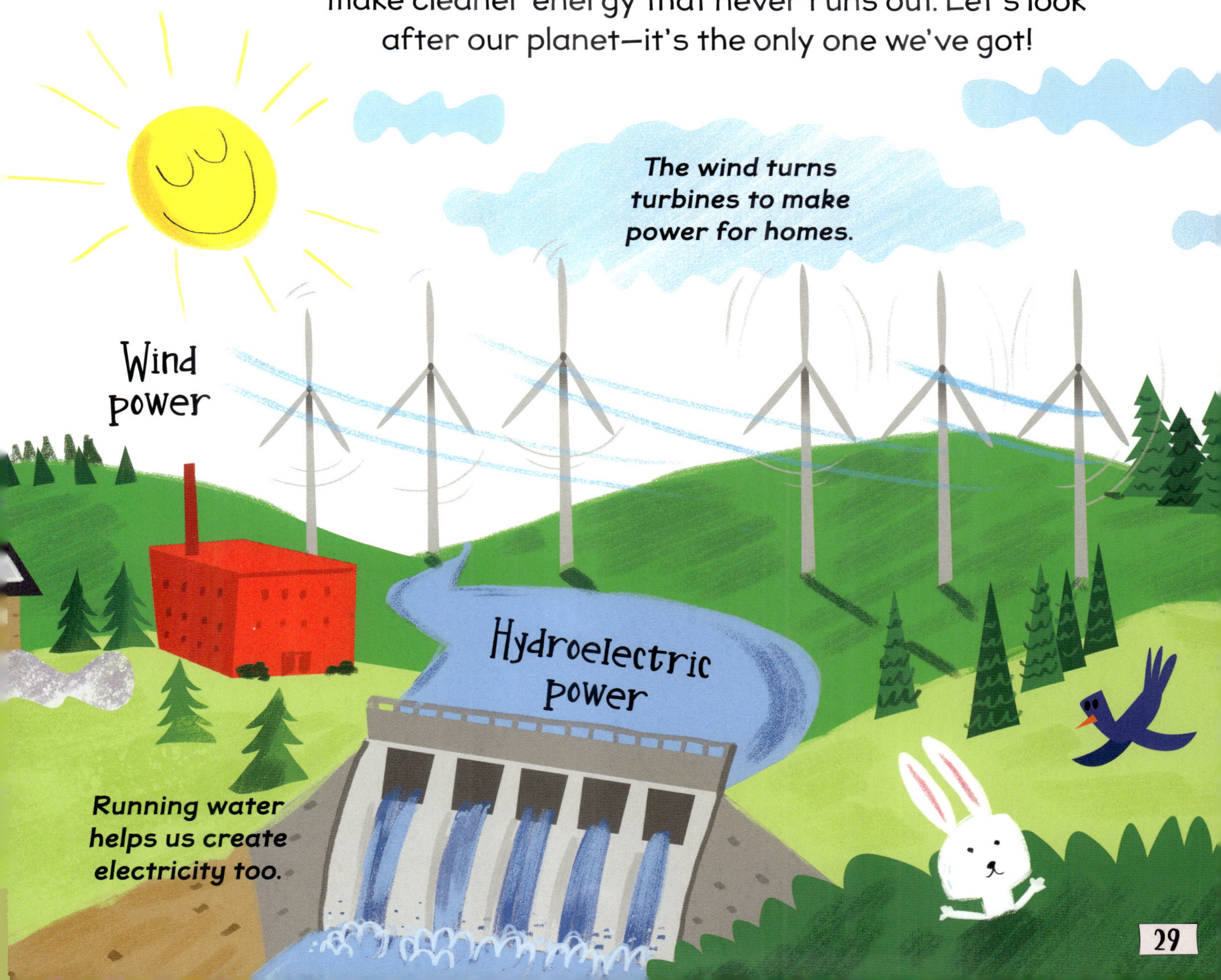

A compendium of questions

Why is rain sometimes red?

Why are hurricanes given names?

It's an easy way of remembering which was which. Famous tropical storms have been called Katrina, Maria, Mitch, and David.

Why do crocodiles like tropical storms?

If it floods, crocodiles can go hunting in the streets. You'd better watch out!

Where is there a special snow festival?

It is held each year in Sapporo, Japan. People make amazing statues and sculptures from ice and snow.

Why do people build houses on stilts?

When it floods in the rainy season in Assam, India, the houses stay high and dry.

Which countries have the worst floods?

India, Bangladesh, and China have had some of the worst floods. This is due to heavy rains, melting snow from high mountains, big rivers, and tropical storms.

Can it really rain frogs or fishes?

Yes! Tiny fish and frogs are sometimes sucked out of ponds and puddles, then fall back to land when it rains.

How do desert animals stay cool?

Many animals burrow underground and only come out at night, when it's cooler. The big ears of the fennec fox help its body to lose heat.

Where are rivers used as roads?

Winters are so cold in Siberia, Russia, that heavy trucks can drive along frozen rivers instead of roads. Milk is sold in solid slabs!

Glossary

buoy an object that floats on a lake, ocean, or another body of water

current a continuous movement of water in the same direction

pressure the weight or force produced when something pushes or pulls against something else

satellite a spacecraft traveling around Earth, a moon, or a planet

tornado a powerful storm in which winds move around a center point

tropical warm and wet

Index